This book is dedicated to my family, friends, mentors, co-workers, the global digital community, and the future generations. Within these pages, there is a blend of the history of the internet, cultural and socio-economic key moments, and bits and bobs from my personal journey.

It bridges 100 years, from 1960 to 2060, linking past, present, and future, and invites curious minds to explore some who's, when's, how's, and why's behind our world's evolution.

The History of the Internet, bits and bobs and beyond

By
Gustavo Morale

INDEX

CHAPTER 1:
A JOURNEY THROUGH DIGITAL TIMES, PERSPECTIVES AND ME

Greetings! I'm Gustavo Morale (known as *Gut* as well) ready to take you on a riveting journey through the evolution of the internet, mixed in with my own story. Born under the effervescent skies of São Paulo, Brazil, on February 3, 1981, I've been privileged to grow up parallel to the digital age, witnessing and "living" the internet morph from its infancy into the colossus it stands as today. And let me tell you, I'm eager to share this wild ride with you, spotlighting not only the internet's key developments but also peering into what the future may unfold. Fasten your seatbelts—it's going to be a thrilling expedition!

Before starting his journey, it is important to understand that this book springs from a deep-rooted fascination and a self-guided odyssey through the realms of the digital age and its intertwining with cultural shifts, a journey enriched by both lived experiences and the ones that eluded my grasp mixed with historical facts regarding technology, economics, cultural and market focused information.

The insights and forecasts unfolding within these pages are carefully crafted from a mix of personal perspectives, in-depth research, and the augmentation of AI, which has empowered me to embark on the journey of writing and publishing my very first book.

Each prediction is infused with a combination of personal reflections and analytical depth. What truly fascinates me, and what I believe will engage the reader, is the seamless narrative journey from 1960 to 2060. It spans a full century, offering a window into the dawn of the digital age. This journey isn't merely a list of technological breakthroughs; it's a vivid exploration of how these developments have reverberated through culture, society, and personal experiences, weaving together a coherent and insightful narrative that spans a transformative era.

Well... The year of my arrival, 1981, wasn't just pivotal because I came into the world... ha ha ha ;) It was a year teeming with global breakthroughs. MTV hit the airwaves, transforming music and pop culture forever. In tandem, the Space Shuttle Columbia blazed a trail into the cosmos, heralding a new era in space exploration. Amidst these milestones, the world grappled with the emergence of a baffling illness later identified as AIDS, and the shock of an assassination attempt on Pope John Paul II. A year marked by technological leaps, cultural shifts, and human resilience.

Back on Brazilian soil, the winds of change were palpable. The nation was amidst the throes of a military dictatorship, yet the seeds of democratisation were beginning to germinate. Economically, Brazil was riding a tumultuous wave, battling inflation and the repercussions of financial overextensions. Despite these hurdles, a sense of optimism and a hunger for advancement were in the air.

Why weave my narrative with the internet's chronicle, you ponder? Simply put, our stories are intricately connected. The internet's trajectory has not only mirrored global shifts but has profoundly impacted our interaction with the world. The debut of the IBM Personal Computer laid the cornerstone for personal computing, while the inaugural space shuttle mission embarked on a journey of celestial discovery. Each of these milestones has, in some way, shaped the digital terrain we navigate today.

Throughout this book, I'll unveil how the internet has sculpted societies, economies, and cultures, revolutionising our modes of communication, entertainment consumption, and much more. We'll delve into pioneering breakthroughs, the tumult of the dot-com bubble, the ascendancy of social media, and the birth of the digital economy. And, we'll venture guesses on future prospects, for in the realm of the internet, the horizons are boundlessly expansive.

So, are you set to plunge into the enthralling universe of the internet, accompanied by a dash of personal tales and a seasoning of historical insight? Let's embark on this adventure together, traversing through the bits and bytes, to unravel the digital revolution that has reshaped our collective human experience.

Amidst these pivotal moments, the world also danced to the tunes of Kim Carnes, whose "Bette Davis Eyes" captivated hearts globally, becoming the year's most adored song. This musical backdrop added another layer to a year that was already rich with technological marvels like the introduction of MS-DOS by Microsoft, setting a new course for personal computing, and the world's first glimpses into the potential of digital graphics and gaming with titles like "Donkey Kong" making their debut.

In this blend of technological innovation and cultural phenomena, my journey began—a narrative interwoven with the threads of global progress and personal growth. Welcome to a tale of digital ascendancy, set against the backdrop of a world coming to grips with its new, interconnected reality.

CHAPTER 2:
HYPERACTIVE WITH FOCUS / PIXELS, DRAWING, CODING, SPORTS, MUSIC AND MAGIC

Back then, calling yourself a nerd didn't come with the cool factor it does today; the term "Geek" wasn't popular yet. It was a whole different vibe, where a mix of digital geekery, artistic flair, and athletic endeavours made up the mosaic of my younger years. I didn't just dip my toes into these interests—as a hyperactive person, a term not used for my generation.

High school was like a treasure hunt, where my curiosity for all things creative and tech took on a life of its own. With a special focus on system analysis and coding, these teachers and subjects became more than just school topics; they formed the foundation of my understanding of logic and structured thinking. By serendipity, this has been a great skill to have throughout my life, providing me with the fluency and capability to engage on a level playing field with diverse specialists from the tech to the creative fields within the digital universe. Between the ages of 15 and 17, it marked the beginning of a thrilling adventure where logic met creativity.

As a hyperactive teenager, the world of drawing and design beckoned with its siren call, pulling me into a realm where I could bring my imaginations to life. Inspired by comic books and artists such as Salvador Dali, Toddy Mcfarlane and Jim Lee, I spent every possible moment sketching and designing, also learning from the best teachers/artists at FIEO's Arts and Design university. This wasn't just a hobby; it was a daily pilgrimage to the altar of creativity and imaginative freedom, where each stroke and colour blend brought me closer to what I was passionate and immersed in.

Gaming, also, played a starring role in my story. The journey began in the 80's with the Intellivision console, an echo from the past that introduced me to a universe of pixelated adventures. While Atari reigned supreme among my friends, my brother and I chose a different path, finding joy and challenge in every game we played. Those long waits for my turn at my cousins'—the youngest of twelve—weren't just downtime. They were my arena, where patience and ambition forged my resolve to dominate each game, making every moment last.

Our appetite for gaming was insatiable, from the enchanting worlds of the Phantom System to the iconic realms of Nintendo, Super Nintendo, Mega Drive, and The PlayStation series. Each new game was a milestone, each challenge a duel, each victory a sweet testament to our dedication.

The realm of RPGs called to me in my early teens, offering epic adventures and fellowship. But the real game-changer was Magic: The Gathering. More than just a card game, it became an all-consuming passion. I was sponsored to play official tournaments, and was part of a crew of players that were travelling and playing together in the Magic The Gathering arena.

But my life wasn't all about gaming, coding and drawing.

Music and art were just as central, weaving together the diverse threads of my youth. My rock band was not a professional band, far from that ;) But it was my outlet for musical expression, another technical code that I challenged myself to break and improve through practice and dedication. I love to accept challenges and tackle problem-solving tasks.

This journey of mine is a celebration of the eclectic hyperactive path well addressed, in my opinion obviously ;) — embracing a wide array of interests, finding harmony in diversity, and discovering the magic that lies in every pursuit. It's a reminder that our passions, no matter how varied, are the foundation of our dreams, the catalysts for lifelong friendships, and the sparks for our future achievements.

I'm aware the details in this chapter might skim the surface, but think of it as setting the stage. Now, let's dive into the heart of the matter ;)

CHAPTER 3:
THE DAWN OF CONNECTIVITY - NAVIGATING THE COLD WAR AND ITS UNFOLDINGS

Stepping back into the weave of our shared story, we exchange the vivid hues of my teenagehood digital awakenings for the grayscale complexity of the 1960s—a period when the world, poised on the brink of technological marvels, was also navigating the murky waters of geopolitical tensions. This segue into the past is not a detour but a journey to the roots of our digital age, set against the backdrop of the Cold War's chessboard, where the stakes were not just global supremacy but the inception of connectivity that would redefine human interaction.

In this era of silent battles and intellectual showdowns, the genesis of the internet emerged as a beacon of innovation— a product of necessity and strategic foresight. As the United States and the Soviet Union played their high-stakes game, the launch of Sputnik in 1957 served as a wake-up call, signalling the urgent need for advancements in communication technology. This spurred the United States to establish ARPA, setting the stage for ARPANET, the precursor to the internet. This network, designed to withstand the unthinkable devastation of nuclear war, introduced the world to the concept of decentralised communication, ensuring that knowledge and information could survive and thrive even in the aftermath of calamity.

Meanwhile, the economic vigour of the post-war era fueled investments in technology and research, laying the groundwork not just for military defence but for a revolution that would touch every aspect of civilian life. The internet, initially a strategic asset, evolved into the backbone of global connectivity, transforming commerce, communication, and community.

The 1960s were not just about silent wars and technological

breakthroughs; they were also the stage for cultural phenomena that captured the world's imagination. The Beatles, with their transcendent melodies and lyrics, became the soundtrack of an era, epitomising change and unity—mirroring the internet's eventual role in bridging disparate worlds.

Transitioning from the global stage to the hallowed halls of MIT, we find ourselves in 1962, at the heart of a revolution that would lay the digital world's foundations. MIT, in those years, was more than an institution; it was a crucible of future-thinking and innovation, where the concept of a globally interconnected network took its first breaths. The air buzzed with potential, as J.C.R. Licklider, or "Lick," envisioned a world linked by computers, heralding the era of global connectivity with his "Galactic Network" concept.

Project MAC epitomised this spirit of innovation, demonstrating the power of shared computing and foreshadowing the collaborative nature of the internet. This pioneering work, though rooted in the academic soil of Cambridge, Massachusetts, was intertwined with the broader objectives of ARPA, showcasing the symbiotic relationship between academia and government in forging the path to the future.

Looking back at this part of history, we see a story made up of innovations, strategy, and cultural evolution—a narrative that highlights how visionary thinking and collaboration can transcend boundaries, connecting us in ways once thought impossible. Amidst the backdrop of the 1960s, the internet emerged as a testament to human ingenuity, a beacon of connectivity that continues to illuminate the path of progress.

CHAPTER 4:
OPENING UP THE DIGITAL STORY
- THE 1970S REVOLUTION

As we glide from the heady days of the 1960s into the vibrant, disco-infused era of the 1970s, the narrative of our journey takes a compelling turn. This chapter isn't just a continuation; it's a celebration of the relentless human spirit, a testament to our insatiable curiosity and our tireless pursuit of connection. The 1970s, with its unique blend of cultural exuberance and technological ambition, served as a crucible for innovations that would further entrench the internet in the fabric of society.

In this period, marked by the rise of bell-bottoms and the hypnotic rhythms of disco, the digital world was taking shape in ways that few could have predicted. The creation of email by Ray Tomlinson in 1971 was a milestone that cannot be overstated. Imagine, for a moment, the sheer novelty of sending a message through a computer network, a concept so revolutionary that it would redefine the boundaries of communication. Email was more than a technological innovation; it was a cultural shift, a bridge across the vastness of space and time, connecting people across the globe with the click of a button.

As the decade progressed, we witnessed the birth of the TCP/IP protocol in 1974, a set of rules that would become the lingua franca of the internet. This was the skeleton key, the code that unlocked the potential for a truly interconnected world. The introduction of this protocol was akin to laying down the railroad tracks for the digital age, establishing a standard that would allow disparate networks to communicate, paving the way for the global network we know today.

Yet, the 1970s were about more than just technical milestones. The era was a melting pot of socio-economic changes, with the digital revolution beginning to hint at its vast potential impacts. The introduction of personal computers towards the latter part of the decade, epitomised by the launch of the Apple II in 1977, democratised computing power, bringing it into homes and offices around the world. This was not merely an evolution; it was a revolution, signalling the start of a new era where the barriers between technology and the everyday person began to blur.

Culturally, the 1970s were defined by the sounds of Led Zeppelin, Pink Floyd, and the soaring harmonies of Fleetwood Mac. Their music, much like the emerging digital technologies, pushed boundaries and challenged conventions, offering a soundtrack to an era of exploration and innovation. The parallels between the disruptive nature of rock and roll and the transformative impact of the internet are uncanny, each in their own way catalysing shifts in societal norms and expectations.

From a marketing perspective, the groundwork laid in the 1970s for digital communication hinted at the dawn of a new era in advertising and consumer engagement. The concept of digital marketing was still in its infancy, but the seeds were planted for a future where brands could connect with consumers through a screen, breaking free from the limitations of traditional media.

The journey from the experimental networks of the 1960s to the burgeoning digital ecosystem of the 1970s is a reminder of the relentless forward march of technology and its ability to reshape our world. As we look back on this era, we're reminded that at the heart of every technological leap forward is a desire to connect, to share, and to understand—a desire that continues to drive the evolution of the internet and the digital landscape.

CHAPTER 5:
NAVIGATING THE DIGITAL CURRENTS
- THE 1980S ODYSSEY

Stepping into the 1980s, we find ourselves riding the crest of a digital wave, one that's swelling with the promise of connectivity and the dawn of a new cultural epoch. This was a decade where neon lights met the burgeoning glow of computer screens, and the rhythm of keyboards syncing with the heartbeat of innovation mirrored the era's defining soundtracks. It was a time when the world began to shrink, not in size, but in the distance between ideas, people, and cultures, thanks to the rapidly evolving landscape of the internet.

The 1980s were marked by a series of groundbreaking milestones in the journey of the internet. The advent of the Domain Name System (DNS) in 1984 transformed the way we navigate the digital world, replacing numerical IP addresses with memorable, human-readable names. This innovation was like laying down the street signs in the burgeoning city of the internet, making it easier for everyone to find their way in the digital expanse.

In the socio-economic sphere, the proliferation of personal computers and the expansion of internet access began to reshape the workplace and the marketplace. The introduction of the IBM PC in 1981, followed by the Apple Macintosh in 1984, ushered in the era of personal computing, democratising access to technology and laying the groundwork for the digital economy. Businesses started to recognize the potential of digital tools for productivity and innovation, sparking a revolution in how work was done and how products were marketed and sold.

Culturally, the 1980s were a vibrant tapestry of music, fashion, and entertainment, all of which were being influenced by the digital revolution. The music of Madonna, Michael Jackson, and Prince, with their synthesiser-driven tracks and boundary-pushing videos, not only defined the sonic landscape of the era but also reflected the growing influence of technology in our lives. These artists, much like the internet itself, were symbols of a new age of expression and connectivity, breaking down barriers and bringing the world closer together.

The impact of the internet on marketing during the 1980s cannot be overstated. As businesses began to explore the potential of digital platforms, we saw the early seeds of what would become digital marketing. Brands started to recognize the power of computers not just as tools for efficiency, but as gateways to new audiences. The concept of reaching consumers through digital channels was still in its infancy, but the foundational ideas for engaging with audiences online were being laid.

As the decade came to a close, the world stood on the precipice of the digital age, with the internet poised to become an integral part of everyday life. The socio-economic implications were profound, heralding a shift towards an information-driven economy and the emergence of new industries centred around digital technologies. Culturally, the fusion of technology and creativity was giving rise to new forms of art, entertainment, and communication, reshaping the cultural landscape in ways that were once unimaginable.

Reflecting on the 1980s, we see a period of transformation and transition, where the dreams of digital pioneers began to crystallise into the reality of a connected world. The milestones of this decade— from the establishment of DNS to the proliferation of personal computers—were not just steps on the path of technological progress; they were leaps towards a future where the internet would become the backbone of global society, economy, and culture. As we navigated the digital currents of the 1980s, we were, in essence, charting the course for the Information Age, setting sail into uncharted waters with the promise of discovery and connection guiding our way.

CHAPTER 6:
SURFING THE DIGITAL WAVE - THE 1990S REVOLUTION

As the calendar flipped to 1990, we were not just entering a new decade; we were stepping into a new realm of possibility. This was the dawn of the '90s, a period that would witness the internet morphing from a niche network for the academically inclined into a cultural phenomenon that touched every corner of society. It was as if we had all been given a ticket to a show we didn't know we were waiting for, and the world eagerly leaned into the glow of their screens, ready to be part of the spectacle.

The early '90s saw the birth of the World Wide Web, thanks to Tim Berners-Lee's vision of a more accessible and interconnected internet. This innovation wasn't just a leap forward; it was a quantum jump that brought the digital universe to the masses. Suddenly, the internet was not just for sending emails or sharing academic papers; it was a vast expanse of information and interaction, a place where anyone with a modem could explore, learn, and connect.

This era also heralded the arrival of web browsers, with Netscape Navigator leading the charge, making the web not just accessible but navigable for the everyday user. The impact was immediate and profound, sparking a digital gold rush as businesses, big and small, scrambled to stake their claim in the online world. The concept of 'dot-com' became synonymous with opportunity, ambition, and for some, a cautionary tale of excess.

The socio-economic landscape of the '90s was fundamentally altered by the rise of the internet. E-commerce emerged as a new frontier, with Amazon and eBay among the pioneers who showed that the web could be a marketplace as well as a meeting place. This shift wasn't just about buying and selling goods online; it was about redefining consumer behaviour, about the convenience and choice that the digital world offered over the brick-and-mortar reality.

Culturally, the '90s were a melting pot, with the internet playing a pivotal role in shaping tastes, trends, and communities. The era's most beloved music, from the grunge of Nirvana to the pop anthems of the Spice Girls, found a new life online, with fans connecting over chat rooms and forums. The internet became a cultural curator, a place where you could discover your next favourite song, movie, or artist, often before they hit the mainstream.

Marketing, too, underwent a transformation in the digital age. The '90s saw the first forays into what would become digital marketing, with brands recognizing the potential of the internet as a platform for reaching audiences in unprecedented ways. Banner ads, email marketing, and, eventually, search engine optimization became tools in the marketer's arsenal, strategies aimed at navigating the vast and growing digital landscape.

As we reflect on the 1990s, it's clear that this was a decade of exploration and expansion. The internet, once a frontier, had become a fixture in daily life, shaping not just how we worked and shopped, but how we connected, created, and consumed culture. It was a time of rapid change, a period when the digital wave swept over us, leaving in its wake a world forever altered.

Looking back, the '90s can be seen as the moment when the internet ceased to be the future and became the present, a fundamental part of the socio-economic fabric, a cultural touchstone, and a marketing marvel. The decade laid the groundwork for the digital age, setting the stage for the innovations, challenges, and opportunities that would come in the new millennium. As we surfed the digital wave of the '90s, we were not just witnesses to history; we were participants in a revolution that redefined what it meant to be connected.

CHAPTER 7:
DREAMS OF THE DIGITAL FRONTIER
- THE DOT-COM SAGA

As we welcomed the year 2000, the digital world was caught in a whirlwind of aspiration and ambition, marking the pinnacle of the dot-com bubble. It was a time when the horizon of internet-centric businesses seemed boundless, fuelled by dreams of endless growth and the tantalising prospect of revolutionising commerce and communication. A cocktail of optimism and the fear of being left behind drove investors to pour immense resources into startups, many of which had little more than a catchy URL and a business plan that was more a leap of faith than a roadmap to financial viability.

This period of frenzy found its apex as the new millennium dawned, with valuations skyrocketing and the NASDAQ, heavy with tech stocks, reaching dizzying heights. Companies adorned with the ".com" badge became the darlings of Wall Street, attracting billions in investment despite often lacking a clear path to profitability or, in some cases, any revenue at all. The internet was celebrated not just as a breakthrough in technology but as a fundamental shift in our economic and social fabric, promising to reshape sectors from retail to media.

However, this bubble was precariously inflated, pumped up by speculative capital and grand expectations that eclipsed the internet's near-term practical applications. The emblematic firms of the dot-com epoch found monetizing their web traffic a Herculean task. The market, initially forgiving of the lack of profitability in anticipation of future growth, began to tighten the screws, demanding concrete results. Doubt seeped in, unravelling the narrative that many of these ventures could live up to their lofty projections, leading to a rapid dissipation of investor confidence.

The dot-com bubble's burst was swift and devastating. By the end of 2000 and into 2001, the NASDAQ Composite took a nosedive, obliterating trillions in market value and spelling the end for countless internet companies. The fallout extended beyond the stock market, triggering job losses, dampening technology investment, and prompting a deep rethinking of the internet's place in business and society.

In the wake of this upheaval, the digital landscape was forever altered. The dot-com crash served as a harsh but necessary lesson, tempering the initial exuberance with a more grounded perspective on the digital realm. Businesses that weathered the storm, and those emerging in its aftermath, recognized the indispensable value of solid business models, profitability, and leveraging technology to meet genuine market demands.

The tale of the dot-com bubble is replete with stories of enterprises that rode the wave of speculative investment to staggering heights, only to plummet back to earth as reality set in. Among these were notable ventures such as:

- Pets.com, the poster child of the era's excess, which evaporated $300 million in funding in its quest to disrupt the pet supply industry online, only to close its doors less than two years after its launch.

- Webvan, with its bold promise to redefine grocery shopping, raced to expand on the strength of $800 million in investment but crumbled under its own weight by 2001.

- eToys.com, once celebrated on the stock market with a valuation in the billions, succumbed to competitive pressures and operational challenges, leading to its bankruptcy in the early 2000s.

- GeoCities, a pioneer in web hosting that Yahoo! acquired for $3.6 billion, struggled with profitability and integration before being shuttered in 2009.

These narratives, spanning from retail and delivery services to web hosting, capture the diverse array of businesses drawn to the internet's potential, yet often ill-prepared for the stark realities of the marketplace. Reflecting on this era, venture capitalists, industry analysts, and the entrepreneurs themselves regard it as a period marked by incredible innovation as well as pivotal lessons in the fundamentals of sustainable business practices. The dot-com bubble stands as a significant chapter in the history of technology and finance, a vivid reminder of the internet's transformative power and the cyclical nature of economic booms and busts.

Music wise, this period witnessed the rise of digital music sharing, notably through platforms like Napster, which fundamentally changed how people accessed and distributed music. Pop and hip-hop dominated the charts, with artists like Britney Spears and NSYNC capturing the hearts of a generation with their catchy tunes and choreographed videos, epitomising the era's pop culture. Simultaneously, hip-hop artists like Jay-Z and Eminem were at the forefront of their genre, both critically and commercially, their lyrics often reflecting the complexities and contradictions of the time. The era was also marked by the emergence of teen pop and boy bands, whose widespread appeal was amplified by the burgeoning internet, making music more accessible to a global audience and setting the stage for the digital music revolution that would follow.

CHAPTER 8:
NAVIGATING THROUGH DIGITAL REBIRTH:
THE INTERNET'S EVOLUTION (2001-2003)

As the calendar turned the page into the 21st century, the internet found itself in uncharted waters. The collapse of the dot-com bubble had left a landscape littered with the remnants of failed ambitions and speculative ventures. Yet, it was within this seeming chaos that the seeds of a profound transformation were sown, marking the dawn of a new era for the digital world. From 2001 to 2003, the internet underwent a metamorphosis, evolving from the speculative frenzy that characterised the late '90s into a structured, sustainable digital economy—a testament to the resilience and innovation inherent in the fabric of the web.

In the immediate aftermath of the market's collapse in 2001, a pivotal innovation emerged that would forever alter the trajectory of online business—the advent of advertising networks. These sophisticated platforms, bridging the gap between advertisers eager to leverage the internet's vast reach and websites in desperate need of sustainable revenue models, revolutionised digital marketing. By enabling targeted advertising with a precision never before seen, these networks not only salvaged floundering online enterprises but also laid the foundation for the monetization strategies that underpin today's digital economy.

As the internet landscape began to stabilise and mature in 2002, the remnants of the '90s' wild west era faded, giving way to a digital marketplace characterised by order and reliability. This shift was marked by enhanced regulatory frameworks and refined business practices, signalling a move towards profitability and sustainability. Companies, from fledgling e-commerce platforms to established content providers, started focusing on delivering real value, fostering a digital ecosystem that was both user-friendly and reliable. This era of digital renaissance attracted a new wave of investment and innovation, bolstering confidence among stakeholders and setting the stage for unprecedented growth.

By the close of 2003, the transformation was undeniable. Over 600 million individuals were now connected to the internet, a milestone that underscored not only the web's rapid adoption but also its integral role in daily life.

This explosion in connectivity, fueled by the spread of broadband access and more affordable computing technology, marked the internet's transition from a niche tool for business and research to a vital component of the global fabric. The web began reshaping everything from how we consume media and communicate to how we learn and participate in civic life.

This period from 2001 to 2003 was more than just a chapter in the history of technology; it was a narrative of rebirth and resilience. The development of advertising networks provided a blueprint for the digital economy's sustainability, while the emergence of a structured internet economy restored faith in the web's potential. The milestone of connecting 600 million people highlighted the internet's expanding influence on global connectivity and community building, laying the groundwork for future innovations and further integration into the essence of everyday existence.

In these years, the digital phoenix rose from the ashes of the dot-com bubble, illustrating the boundless potential of the internet even in the face of adversity. The early 2000s were not just a time of recovery but a period of reimagining and reinvention, proving that from the greatest challenges can emerge the most profound opportunities for growth and innovation. As we reflect on this era of digital renaissance, we recognize it as the foundation upon which the modern internet was built—a testament to the enduring power of human creativity and the unassailable spirit of the digital age.

CHAPTER 9: THE SOCIAL NETWORKS (2004)

In the early dawn of the 21st century, the digital world found itself on the cusp of a transformative era, one that would expand the horizons of connectivity and forge new paths for social interaction. The year 2004, in particular, emerged as a defining milestone, marking the rise of social networking sites that would weave a new fabric into the socio-economic structure of the internet. This evolution was not merely a technological leap but a redefinition of how communities were built, how voices were shared, and how the world was connected.

The launch of Facebook from the confines of a Harvard dormitory encapsulated this shift. What began as a localised platform for college students rapidly transcended its initial scope, evolving into a global phenomenon that connected diverse voices across continents. Facebook's ascendancy to the global stage was symbolic of the broader emergence of social media as a vital tool for human connection, leveraging the internet's expansive reach to fulfil a basic human need for interaction and belonging.

Yet, the narrative of social networking's ascent is not solely the story of Facebook. This era saw the proliferation of various platforms, each contributing uniquely to the tapestry of online social interaction. LinkedIn, for instance, redefined professional networking by facilitating connections based on career interests and backgrounds, transforming the landscape of professional opportunities and career development. Similarly, Flickr's integration of photo-sharing with social networking elements highlighted the evolving dynamics of online interaction, where shared interests and passions could foster communities.

This burgeoning social network landscape profoundly influenced the socio-economic dynamics of the digital age. Businesses swiftly recognized the potential of these platforms for targeted marketing, customer engagement, and brand awareness. The concept of viral marketing found fertile ground here, with the interconnected nature of social networks allowing for rapid dissemination of content. Moreover, the wealth of data generated by user interactions on these platforms offered unprecedented insights into consumer behaviour, preferences, and trends, revolutionising marketing strategies and product development.

The introduction and rapid global adoption of social networking sites in 2004 signified more than just the expansion of digital communication; it heralded a new epoch in the interplay between technology, economy, and society. These platforms reshaped the business landscape, introducing novel models for interaction and commerce, and became woven into the very essence of the internet, influencing societal norms and practices.

However, the ascent of social networking also brought to light challenges, including concerns over privacy, data security, and the spread of misinformation. These issues underscored the complexities of the digital social landscape, prompting discussions on regulation, governance, and ethical responsibility among platform operators.

Reflecting on this pivotal period, it's clear that 2004 marked the dawn of an era where the internet became intrinsically social, fundamentally altering the way people connect, communicate, and consume content. This chapter in the digital saga set the stage for the intertwined future of social media and society, showcasing the lasting impact of connectivity and community in shaping the modern world. As we look back on this transformative phase, the legacy of social networking's rise continues to influence not just the technology sector but society at large, dictating the rhythms of daily life, commerce, and global discourse in the digital age.

CHAPTER 10:
PASSION AND ENTREPRENEURSHIP
(2001 / 2006 / 2016)

Back in the early 2000s, when the digital cosmos was just stretching its wings, I found myself stepping into the halls of PUC São Paulo, my heart set on conquering the world of Social Communications, Advertising, and Propaganda. I was 20, buzzing with the kind of energy that could light up a city, already dipping my toes in the work pool at a communication agency. Those were the days of selling dreams in the guise of ads, of crafting designs that whispered sweet nothings into the consumer's ear.

A door swung open when a teacher nudged me towards an opportunity that smelled of adventure and espresso—Benetton's Fabrica in Treviso, Italy. The selection process was a marathon, not a sprint, testing my patience and resolve over 12 long months. English, the key I lacked, became my mission. Juggling work, studies, and a fiery determination to break language barriers, I saved every penny for a ticket to Australia. Perth was my battlefield, where I traded sweat for fluency, under the watchful eyes and unwavering support of my family. Yet, destiny had its own script. Benetton's "no" hit me like a winter chill. Disappointment was a bitter pill, but it brewed a realisation within me—the pursuit of a dream, even if unfulfilled, moulds you in unimaginable ways.

Shaking off the dust, I found myself as a Digital Art Director back in São Paulo. But as fate would have it, the agency's founders were great but they had a peculiar habit of forgetting paydays. Three months in, I walked away, a question burning in my mind: "If they could do it, why not me? I will make it much better!"

Thus began my dance with entrepreneurship, a laboratory of organic experiences. The WhiteCat was born out of a college brainstorm with Fabio Moran, a kindred spirit from university. Together, we embarked on a digital odyssey, painting brands' dreams across the virtual canvas, from logo designs to full-fledged digital campaigns. I'm very grateful for the experience I have had, working with great friends between creative directors, designers and clients. Our little agency was a crucible of creativity and technology studies, focused on bradining, illustration and mainly impactful Dynamic Flash websites, and creative campaigns, churning out over thirty projects for a kaleidoscope of clients in 4 years. Those were the days of pure adrenaline, of making something very special from entrepreneurial call.

The plot thickened in 2006. Post-MBA and with a heavy heart, I bid adieu to The WhiteCat, yet, the entrepreneurial fire within me was far from extinguished. Alongside Marco Santos, a friend and tech wizard, and other co-founders, we launched HOTWords contextual advertising, one of Latin America's pioneering AdNetworks. Our digital brainchild soared, touching the lives of over 92% of Brazil's internet users, democratising digital advertising, and carving a niche in the hearts of content creators across the region. This dream turned mine and other people's life to a unique experience, making trainees into directors, talented hard working professionals from São Paulo and Brazil were made this project fly like a few.

Explaining the journey from founding HOTWords contextual advertising to evolving into Media Response Group encapsulates a monumental chapter in my career, almost demanding a book of its own. In 2009 VSS alongside Canal Mail Spain acquired the company, which had originated The Media Response Group. This period, stretching over a decade, feels like a distinct lifetime, filled with achievements I hold in high esteem. Among these, all friends and memorable moments lived. A successful company that was able to monetize over 35,000 publishers across nine countries for a span of ten years generating revenue based on advertising campaigns served on their pages. The experiences gained, the diverse and exceptional array of people I worked alongside —friends, co-workers, and more—have enriched this journey, making it a memorable key moment of my life.

Reflecting on this rollercoaster, not just for the business milestones, but for the journey, for the people whose lives we touched, for the digital trail we blazed across Latin America, Europe and North America. This chapter of my life, intertwined with the digital tapestry of the era, is a testament to the power of dreams, the resilience required to chase them, and the profound impact one can have on the world's digital stage. It's a narrative of navigating the digital revolution, and ultimately, of leaving a legacy that resonates far beyond the confines of boardrooms and balance sheets. Maybe this could be my next book.

CHAPTER 11:
ABOVE 1 BILLION GLOBAL USERS CONNECTED
& THE IPHONE RELEASE (2007)

In 2007, the digital tapestry of our world was irrevocably changed, marked by two monumental shifts that would redefine global connectivity and personal technology. This year saw the number of people connected to the internet soar to an astonishing 1.234 billion, a testament to the web's expanding role as a fundamental aspect of daily life across the globe. But perhaps even more transformative was the introduction of a device that would become an extension of our very selves: the iPhone. This convergence of increased internet connectivity and the dawn of the smartphone revolution set the stage for a new era in the socio-economic landscape, the effects of which continue to shape our current age.

The surge in internet connectivity in 2007 was not merely a numerical milestone; it represented a profound shift in the way information was accessed, shared, and disseminated. For the first time, a significant portion of the global population could tap into the vast reservoir of knowledge, connect with others across continents in real-time, and participate in the digital economy, regardless of geographical boundaries. This democratisation of access had far-reaching implications for education, commerce, and social interaction, laying the groundwork for a more interconnected world.

Simultaneously, the launch of the iPhone by Apple Inc. catalysed the smartphone revolution, forever altering our relationship with technology. The iPhone was not just a phone; it was a powerful computer, a camera, a portal to the internet, and a platform for applications that could perform an endless variety of functions.

Its intuitive design and groundbreaking touch interface made advanced technology accessible to the masses, setting a new standard for personal devices. The smartphone became the primary means of internet access for millions, accelerating the spread of digital connectivity and fostering a mobile-first world.

The impact of these developments on our current age is profound and multifaceted. The widespread adoption of smartphones, coupled with increased internet connectivity, has fueled the rise of social media, changed the face of commerce with the advent of mobile banking and e-commerce, and revolutionised how we consume media. It has also enabled new forms of work and collaboration, with remote and flexible working arrangements becoming increasingly feasible and popular.

Moreover, the data generated by billions of connected individuals and devices has given rise to the era of big data, with analytics and machine learning offering insights that drive decision-making in business, healthcare, and governance. However, this digital integration has also raised important questions about privacy, data security, and the digital divide, highlighting the challenges that accompany our connected world.

The year 2007 stands as a pivotal point in the digital chronicle, a year that saw the fusion of enhanced global connectivity with the advent of the smartphone, setting the foundation for the deeply digital, interconnected life we live today. The socio-economic ramifications of these shifts are still unfolding, as we navigate the benefits and challenges of a world where the internet and smartphones continue to reshape every aspect of our society.

CHAPTER 12:
MARKETING UPGRADE - ROI, CONTENT
AND RETARGETING (2008-2010)

As the late 2000s unfolded, the digital marketing landscape underwent a transformative evolution, marking a period where the principles governing online success were redefined. The years from 2008 to 2010 were characterised by a series of paradigm shifts that would not only redefine strategies but also set new benchmarks for measuring success in the digital domain.

The year 2008 heralded the era where Return on Investment (ROI) became the cornerstone of digital marketing strategies. Amidst the economic uncertainties of the time, businesses began to scrutinise every dollar spent, with a heightened focus on the tangible outcomes of their marketing efforts. This shift towards ROI-centric strategies marked a significant departure from the earlier, more experimental approaches to digital marketing. Companies started to demand more accountability, seeking clear correlations between marketing expenditures and financial returns. The digital marketing world responded with more sophisticated analytics and measurement tools, enabling marketers to prove the efficacy of their campaigns in real, quantifiable terms.

As the focus on ROI solidified its place in the marketing playbook, the year 2009 brought with it the realisation that content was, indeed, king. This was a time when the quality of online content emerged as a critical determinant of success. Search engines began to prioritise relevant, high-quality content in their rankings, compelling businesses to rethink their content strategies. This period underscored the importance of creating valuable, engaging, and informative content that resonated with audiences. It wasn't just about attracting eyes; it was about holding attention, fostering engagement, and building trust. Quality content became the currency of the digital realm, driving traffic, generating leads, and establishing brand authority.

The dawn of the 2010s witnessed the advent of retargeting technology, adding a new dimension to online advertising strategies. Retargeting revolutionised the way businesses approached potential customers, allowing them to 'follow' users across the web with targeted ads based on previous interactions. This technology was a game-changer, significantly increasing conversion rates by keeping brands top-of-mind and effectively re-engaging visitors who had not made an immediate purchase. The introduction of retargeting technology marked a shift towards more personalised and persistent marketing efforts, leveraging data and user behaviour to tailor marketing messages more effectively.

These pivotal years in the late 2000s and early 2010s reshaped the digital marketing landscape, setting new standards for success and introducing technologies that remain at the core of digital strategies today. The emphasis on ROI, the prioritisation of quality content, and the innovative use of retargeting technology have all played fundamental roles in crafting the modern digital marketing playbook. These developments not only enhanced the effectiveness of online marketing but also fostered a more dynamic and responsive interaction between brands and their audiences. As we navigate the current age of digital marketing, the impact of these milestones continues to influence strategies, guiding marketers in their quest to connect, engage, and convert in an ever-evolving digital world.

CHAPTER 13: DECENTRALISING THE FUTURE - THE CRYPTOCURRENCY REVOLUTION AND ITS IMPACT ON THE DIGITAL AGE (2009)

In the grand tapestry of the digital age, few threads are as vivid and transformative as the emergence of cryptocurrencies. It's a story that begins in 2009, not with a bang, but with the quiet, revolutionary whisper of Bitcoin's creation. Behind the pseudonym Satoshi Nakamoto, an individual or group laid the cornerstone for what would become a seismic shift in our global financial systems.

Imagine, for a moment, a world where the control of money isn't tethered to towering institutions or bound by national borders. That's the promise of Bitcoin—a decentralised digital currency that operates on trust in mathematics rather than the word of banks or governments. It's akin to discovering a new continent in the digital realm, untouched by the traditional powers that be.

As Bitcoin's whispers grew into conversations, then into loud, global discussions, it wasn't alone for long. Come 2015, Ethereum entered the stage, broadening the narrative. Ethereum wasn't just another digital currency; it was a platform, a framework upon which more complex, automated transactions could be built, thanks to smart contracts. It's as if, after discovering a new continent, someone started distributing tools to build whatever you could imagine on it.

The socio-economic impact of these digital currencies has been profound. For starters, they've democratised investing. No longer is the world of lucrative investments gated behind wealth or insider knowledge. With cryptocurrencies, anyone with an internet connection could participate, leading to stories of overnight millionaires and, admittedly, tales of losses just as rapidly. But beyond the volatile market charts, cryptocurrencies have sparked a global conversation about the nature of money itself and who gets to control it.

This conversation couldn't be more timely. In a world where privacy often feels like an endangered concept, cryptocurrencies offer a veil of anonymity. They've become the digital age's response to a growing desire for privacy and control over one's financial destiny, challenging the narrative that our financial lives must be an open book for banks and governments.

However, with great power comes great scrutiny. Regulators, financial institutions, and investors have turned their gaze toward cryptocurrencies, drawn by their potential and propelled by the need to understand and sometimes contain their impact. The dance between innovation and regulation is a delicate one, playing out on a global stage. It's a strategic pivot point, where the future of finance is being negotiated, not in closed boardrooms, but in open forums, development labs, and marketplaces across the world.

The strategic perspective on this tale of digital currencies is clear: we're at the cusp of a financial renaissance. Cryptocurrencies are more than a technological novelty; they are a challenge to the status quo, a test of our existing financial paradigms. As we look forward to 2024, the question isn't just about how cryptocurrencies will evolve, but how they will reshape the landscape of global finance, privacy, and individual autonomy.

In weaving this chapter into the larger narrative of the digital age, it's evident that cryptocurrencies are not just a footnote. They are a bold declaration of the potential for innovation to redefine the boundaries of what's possible. As we chart the course of the digital era, the story of Bitcoin, Ethereum, and the myriad of digital currencies is a reminder of the power of ideas to challenge, transform, and occasionally, revolutionise the world.

So, as we venture forward, the legacy of cryptocurrencies stands as a beacon, illuminating the path toward a future where finance is more inclusive, transparent, and, most importantly, under the stewardship of the many rather than the few. It's a chapter still being written, but one that promises to be as compelling as any in the saga of our digital age.

CHAPTER 14:
REVOLUTIONISING THE DIGITAL LANDSCAPE: CONNECTIVITY, INNOVATION, AND THE RISE OF DATA (2011-2013)

As we ventured deeper into the second decade of the 21st century, the digital landscape underwent a period of unprecedented growth and transformation. The years between 2011 and 2013 were marked by significant advancements in technology and digital marketing, reshaping the socio-economic fabric of the internet and laying the groundwork for a new digital ecosystem.

In 2011, the digital advertising world witnessed the establishment of ad exchanges, a pivotal development that revolutionised online advertising. Ad exchanges created a dynamic marketplace where advertisers and publishers could buy and sell advertising space in real-time through automated bidding. This innovation democratised access to advertising inventory, optimised the allocation of digital ad space, and injected a new level of efficiency and transparency into the digital advertising market. The advent of ad exchanges marked a departure from traditional, negotiation-based ad buying, paving the way for a more fluid, data-driven approach to digital marketing.

The following year, 2012, was notable for two significant milestones that further accelerated the digital revolution. Firstly, global internet connectivity reached a new zenith, with 2.4 billion people connected to the internet. This surge in connectivity not only expanded the digital audience but also amplified the potential for digital engagements, e-commerce, and information exchange on an unprecedented scale. Secondly, 2012 was characterised by ultra technological advancements that fostered a new digital ecosystem. Innovations in mobile technology, cloud computing, and social media platforms transformed the way individuals interacted with digital content, each other, and brands online. These advancements expanded the digital landscape, creating new opportunities for marketing, communication, and business models that leveraged the burgeoning connectivity and technological capabilities.

By 2013, the mantra "Data is King" had taken hold, signifying the rise of big data analytics and programmatic advertising. The ability to collect, analyse, and act on vast amounts of data in real-time revolutionised marketing strategies, allowing for unprecedented targeting and personalization. Programmatic advertising, powered by big data analytics, automated the decision-making process of ad placements, utilising complex algorithms to deliver the right message to the right user at the right time. This shift towards data-driven marketing strategies underscored the importance of data as a critical asset in the digital age, enabling marketers to optimise campaigns, enhance user experiences, and improve ROI through targeted and personalised advertising.

The period from 2011 to 2013 was a transformative era that reshaped the digital domain, driven by technological innovations, increased global connectivity, and the ascendancy of data analytics. The establishment of ad exchanges, the explosive growth in internet users, the emergence of a new digital ecosystem, and the rise of big data and programmatic advertising collectively propelled the digital economy forward. These developments not only influenced marketing practices but also had profound socio-economic implications, affecting how businesses operated, how consumers accessed information and products, and how society at large engaged with the digital world. As we reflect on this pivotal chapter in digital history, it's clear that these years laid the foundation for the sophisticated, interconnected, and data-driven digital landscape we navigate today.

CHAPTER 15:
HARMONISING THE DIGITAL SYMPHONY:
THE MOBILE REVOLUTION AND
STREAMING ERA (2013-2015)

In the heart of the second decade of the 21st century, the digital world experienced a symphonic blend of innovation, connectivity, and mobility, crafting a new rhythm to which the global population danced. The period from 2013 to 2015 was marked by significant advancements that not only transformed user behaviour but also reshaped the socio-economic landscape of the digital ecosystem.

The rise of audio streaming services, spearheaded by platforms like Spotify in 2013, marked the beginning of a seismic shift in how music was consumed. Gone were the days of physical albums and even downloads; the era of instant, on-demand access to millions of songs was upon us. Spotify and its contemporaries offered a personalised music experience, leveraging algorithms to recommend music based on listening habits, thus introducing a novel way of discovering and enjoying music. This evolution in music consumption reflected broader trends towards personalization and convenience, underscoring the internet's role in democratising access to content.

By 2014, the proclamation that "Mobile is King" captured the essence of the internet's evolution. For the first time, mobile platforms overtook desktops in terms of internet usage, a milestone that underscored the shift towards a more personal, immediate, and on-the-go digital experience. Smartphones became the primary gateway to the internet for billions, embodying the convergence of communication, entertainment, and information in the palm of one's hand. This mobile dominance spurred innovations in app development, responsive design, and mobile marketing, compelling businesses to rethink their digital strategies to meet users where they were: on their phones.

The following year, 2015, witnessed the ascent of live streaming platforms, with Periscope leading the charge. Live streaming brought a new dimension to online content, offering real-time engagement that bridged the gap between content creators and audiences. This immediacy and authenticity attracted users and opened new avenues for content creation, marketing, and social interaction. The ability to broadcast and consume live content from anywhere in the world emphasised the internet's power to connect people in unprecedented ways.

Simultaneously, the global internet user base continued to swell, reaching 3.2 billion people in 2015. This exponential growth in connectivity not only highlighted the internet's expanding reach but also its role as a critical infrastructure underpinning modern society. Each new user represented a node in an increasingly dense web of global interactions, contributing to the rich tapestry of the digital world.

The period between 2013 and 2015 was a testament to the rapid pace of digital innovation and its profound impact on society, culture, and the economy. The emergence of audio streaming services, the dominance of mobile platforms, the rise of live streaming, and the continued growth in global internet connectivity together wove a new narrative in the digital age. This narrative was characterised by enhanced access to content, the ubiquity of mobile devices, and the power of real-time communication, shaping a future where digital experiences are increasingly personalised, immediate, and interconnected. As we reflect on this transformative period, it's clear that these developments were not just fleeting trends but pivotal moments that continue to influence the digital landscape, echoing through the ways we live, work, and connect in the digital age.

CHAPTER 16:
NAVIGATING NEW REALITIES: FROM VIRTUAL SPACES TO VOICE COMMANDS (2016-2018)

As we ventured deeper into the second decade of the 21st century, the digital landscape continued to evolve at an unprecedented pace, marked by groundbreaking advancements and shifts that would redefine the interaction between technology and society. The years between 2016 and 2018 were a testament to the rapid innovation that characterises our era, witnessing the rise of virtual and augmented realities, the integration of artificial intelligence in everyday interactions, the emergence of influencer marketing as a dominant force, the tightening of data privacy regulations, and the advent of voice search and smart speakers.

In 2016, the digital world buzzed with excitement over the advancements in Virtual Reality (VR) and Augmented Reality (AR) technologies. This period saw VR and AR move beyond the realms of niche gaming and tech enthusiasts to mainstream consciousness, offering immersive experiences that blurred the lines between the physical and digital worlds. Brands and marketers quickly recognized the potential of these technologies to create compelling, interactive narratives, transforming the way products and experiences were showcased.

The following year, 2017, heralded the increased integration of Artificial Intelligence (AI) and chatbots in customer service, signalling a shift towards more personalised, efficient consumer interactions. AI-driven chatbots began to handle a wide range of tasks, from answering frequently asked questions to providing personalised shopping advice, significantly enhancing the customer experience while streamlining operations for businesses.

Simultaneously, 2017 marked the rise of influencer marketing, a trend fueled by the growing clout of social media personalities. Influencers, with their dedicated followings and perceived authenticity, became coveted partners for brands looking to tap into niche audiences. This form of marketing underscored the shifting dynamics of trust and recommendation in the digital age, with peer influence often outweighing traditional advertising in effectiveness.

In 2018, the digital world encountered a significant regulatory milestone with the implementation of the General Data Protection Regulation (GDPR) in the European Union. GDPR represented a major step forward in data privacy and protection, setting stringent guidelines for the collection, storage, and use of personal information. Its impact was global, prompting companies worldwide to reassess their data handling practices and prioritise user privacy, reshaping the relationship between businesses and consumers in the digital domain.

That same year, the proliferation of smart speakers and the rise of voice-activated assistants highlighted a significant shift towards voice search and command as a primary mode of interacting with technology. This development signalled a move towards more natural, intuitive user interfaces, opening up new avenues for content delivery, search engine optimization, and consumer engagement.

The period from 2016 to 2018 was characterised by rapid technological evolution and changing consumer expectations, driving businesses and marketers to adapt in real-time. The advancements in VR and AR, the integration of AI and chatbots, the rise of influencer marketing, the enactment of GDPR, and the advent of voice search and smart speakers collectively painted a picture of a digital landscape in constant flux. These years not only redefined the tools and strategies at the disposal of digital marketers but also set new standards for privacy, interactivity, and user engagement, charting the course for the future of digital innovation and its socio-economic impact.

CHAPTER 17: NEW BEGINNINGS
IN LONDON (2017)

2017 marked the beginning of a significant new chapter in my life, one that would see me and my family embark on a transformative journey far from the familiar landscapes of São Paulo. After years of navigating the ever-evolving digital market in our home country, pushing boundaries, and contributing to the vibrant tapestry of its digital evolution, the decision to move abroad crystallised into reality. London called, and with a mix of excitement and anticipation, we answered, choosing this historic and dynamic city as the new backdrop for our family's story.

The move to London was driven by a multitude of aspirations, foremost among them the desire to provide our son with unparalleled opportunities for education and personal growth. London, with its rich cultural heritage, diversity, and world-renowned academic institutions, presented itself as the ideal setting for nurturing his potential. But beyond the ambitions we harboured for our son, the relocation was also about fulfilling a personal dream of mine — to immerse myself in a new environment, to start from scratch, and to experience the personal and professional growth that comes from stepping into the unknown.

Starting anew in London was as challenging as it was exhilarating. The initial years were a tapestry of learning and adaptation, of embracing the lifestyle and rhythms of a city vastly different from what we had known. The transition was not merely geographical; it represented a shift in mindset, a redefinition of our family's narrative, and a broadening of our horizons. London, with its eclectic mix of history and modernity, tradition and innovation, quickly endeared itself to us, offering a lifestyle that was both enriching and invigorating.

Now, seven years into this journey, I can confidently say that London has become much more than just a new home. It has become a source of inspiration, a place where the vibrancy of city life merges seamlessly with the tranquillity of its green spaces, where the global meets the local in a dynamic dance of cultures and ideas. The decision to move here has been vindicated by the experiences we've had, the friendships we've formed, and the personal and professional growth we've undergone.

Professionally, London offered a fresh canvas for my digital marketing expertise. The city's status as a global hub for innovation and its thriving digital sector provided new avenues for exploration and contribution. The challenges of establishing oneself in a new market were met with the opportunities to engage with diverse perspectives, to learn from the cutting-edge of digital innovation, and to bring my experiences from Brazil and Latin America to bear in a new context.

This chapter of our lives, set against the backdrop of London's vibrant landscape, has been a testament to the power of change, the value of new experiences, and the endless possibilities that come with embracing a new beginning. It's a narrative of personal and professional evolution, of building a life in a city that continues to inspire and challenge us in equal measure. As I reflect on these seven years, I'm filled with gratitude for the journey thus far and anticipation for the chapters yet to unfold in this incredible city that we now call home.

CHAPTER 18:
NAVIGATING THE NEW NORMS OF CONNECTIVITY AND COMMERCE

As the second decade of the 21st century drew to a close, a series of pivotal developments unfolded, reshaping the socio-economic and marketing landscapes in profound ways. The onset of 2019 marked the dawn of the 5G era, setting the stage for a transformative leap in global connectivity. This period also witnessed the unforeseen challenges brought about by the COVID-19 pandemic in 2020, catalysing a seismic shift in work habits, consumer behaviour, and digital engagement across the globe.

The global rollout of 5G technology heralded a new age of internet connectivity, promising unprecedented speeds and reliability that could support the next generation of digital innovation. This technological advancement was not just about faster internet; it was a cornerstone for the burgeoning Internet of Things (IoT), smart cities, and a host of other futuristic applications. Marketers and businesses alike eyed the potential of 5G to revolutionise consumer experiences, from augmented reality shopping to real-time, ultra-high-definition content streaming.

However, as 5G networks began their gradual expansion across the globe, the world was bracing for a challenge of monumental scale — the outbreak of the COVID-19 pandemic. The year 2020 became a watershed moment for society and the economy, as health concerns necessitated widespread lockdowns and social distancing measures. This new reality propelled remote work and video conferencing to the forefront of daily life, fundamentally altering the way businesses operate and how people interact. Platforms like Zoom, Microsoft Teams, and Google Meet became household names almost overnight, enabling not just business continuity but also keeping friends and families connected in a time of isolation.

The pandemic's impact on digital connectivity was equally staggering. By 2020, the number of internet users surged to 4.1 billion people, driven by the increased reliance on digital platforms for work, education, entertainment, and shopping. This growth underscored the internet's role as a lifeline during the crisis, highlighting the critical need for robust digital infrastructures and accessible online services.

Another notable trend that gained momentum in this period was the explosive growth of e-sports and online gaming. With traditional sports events and social gatherings on pause, millions turned to digital platforms for entertainment and community. E-sports tournaments attracted viewership numbers that rivalled those of conventional sports, while online gaming platforms became virtual social hubs. This surge not only provided a much-needed outlet for connection and competition but also opened new avenues for marketers to engage with highly engaged audiences through in-game advertising and sponsorships.

These developments, from the rollout of 5G networks to the shifts induced by the COVID-19 pandemic, have indelibly shaped the socio-economic fabric of our world. They have propelled digital connectivity to new heights, redefined the norms of work and social interaction, and opened up innovative pathways for marketing and commerce. As we navigate this ever-evolving digital landscape, the lessons and opportunities born out of these pivotal years continue to influence strategies, policies, and visions for a connected future. In this era of digital horizons, we are reminded of the resilience, adaptability, and transformative potential of our global society.

CHAPTER 19:
REVEALING THE DIGITAL MOSAIC.
THE RISE OF NFTS, AUGMENTED
REALITY AND THE METAVERSE

In the early 2020s, the digital world witnessed a series of groundbreaking shifts that would further redefine the socio-economic and marketing landscapes. The years 2021 and 2022, in particular, marked the onset of significant technological phenomena, including the explosive popularity of Non-Fungible Tokens (NFTs), a surge in cryptocurrency adoption, and an increased focus on the Metaverse and extended reality. Furthermore, the era saw the dominance of short-form video content, with platforms like TikTok revolutionising how content is consumed and created.

The year 2021 was notably marked by the NFT and cryptocurrency boom. NFTs emerged from the digital shadows to become a cultural and economic sensation, allowing artists, creators, and collectors to monetize digital art and assets in ways previously unimaginable. This boom was underpinned by blockchain technology, which provided a secure, decentralised ledger for recording the ownership and transfer of these unique digital items. Similarly, cryptocurrencies saw an unprecedented rise in adoption, both as an investment asset and a means of transaction. Businesses and marketers quickly recognized the potential of integrating blockchain technology into their operations, from offering crypto payments to leveraging NFTs for marketing campaigns, thus opening new avenues for digital ownership and commerce.

As 2022 unfolded, the digital narrative expanded to encompass the Metaverse and extended reality (XR), concepts that promised a new dimension of online interaction. The Metaverse, a collective virtual shared space created by the convergence of virtually enhanced physical and digital reality, became a buzzword across industries, heralding a future where digital experiences are as integral to our lives as physical ones. This focus on extended reality — encompassing virtual reality (VR), augmented reality (AR), and mixed reality (MR) — signalled a shift towards more immersive digital experiences. Businesses, educators, and marketers began exploring these technologies to create engaging, interactive environments for consumers, students, and audiences, blurring the lines between the digital and physical worlds.

Another defining trend of this period was the rise of short-form video content, with TikTok leading the charge. This platform transformed the content creation landscape, enabling users to produce and share bite-sized videos that could go viral overnight. The immediacy and accessibility of short-form video content catered to the decreasing attention spans of digital audiences, offering a new formula for engagement and virality. Marketers quickly adapted to this trend, leveraging platforms like TikTok for brand campaigns, influencer partnerships, and user-generated content initiatives, thereby tapping into the platform's vast and highly engaged user base.

These developments, from the NFT and cryptocurrency explosion to the advent of the Metaverse and the popularity of short-form video content, have significantly impacted socio-economic dynamics and marketing strategies. They have introduced new paradigms for digital commerce, content consumption, and online interaction, highlighting the fluid and ever-evolving nature of the digital ecosystem. As we navigate through this unfolding digital tapestry, the implications of these trends continue to resonate, shaping the future of digital engagement, commerce, and creativity. In this era of constant digital innovation, staying at the forefront of these shifts is paramount for businesses, creators, and marketers aiming to harness the full potential of the digital realm.

CHAPTER 20:
AI-GENERATED CONTENT AND THE QUANTUM LEAP

As we venture deeper into the 2020s, the frontier of digital innovation continues to expand, revealing new possibilities and challenges that redefine the socio-economic and marketing landscapes. The years 2023 and the projections for 2024 stand as pivotal chapters in this ongoing narrative, marked by significant advancements in artificial intelligence (AI) for content creation and the anticipated influence of quantum computing on internet technology.

In 2023, the realm of AI-generated content emerged as a powerful force, reshaping the way we conceive, create, and consume digital content. AI technologies have evolved to produce written articles, generate creative artwork, compose music, and even script videos, blurring the lines between human and machine creativity. This surge in AI-driven content creation tools has democratised content production, enabling marketers, bloggers, artists, and small businesses to generate high-quality content at scale, reducing costs and time-to-market. The implications of this shift are profound, offering opportunities for personalised and dynamic content strategies that can adapt to the real-time preferences and behaviours of audiences.

As we look at the projected advancements in 2024, the horizon is illuminated by the potential emergence of quantum computing and its impact on internet technology. Quantum computing promises computational powers vastly exceeding those of current binary computing systems, offering the ability to process complex data at unprecedented speeds. This leap in computing capability is poised to revolutionise various sectors, including cryptography, data analysis, and the very infrastructure of the internet. For the digital economy, quantum computing could enhance the capabilities of AI, enable more sophisticated data encryption methods, and potentially introduce new internet protocols that could further secure digital communications.

The intersection of AI-generated content and quantum computing heralds a new era of digital innovation, where the creation, distribution, and security of content are undergoing radical transformations. Marketers and businesses are presented with both challenges and opportunities as they navigate this evolving landscape. The ability to leverage AI for content creation opens up new avenues for engaging with audiences, requiring a reevaluation of traditional content strategies and the ethical considerations surrounding AI-generated materials. Simultaneously, the advent of quantum computing invites a reimagining of data security, privacy, and the overall architecture of digital platforms.

These developments underscore a period of rapid technological change, prompting a reexamination of how we interact with the digital world and the tools we use to connect, communicate, and conduct business. As we approach these new frontiers, the need for agility, foresight, and ethical consideration becomes increasingly paramount. Businesses, creators, and marketers must stay attuned to these advancements, embracing the potential of AI and quantum computing while navigating the complex questions they pose. In this dynamic digital era, the ability to adapt and innovate is key to unlocking new possibilities and thriving in the ever-changing digital landscape.

CHAPTER 21:
CHARTING A COURSE TOWARD
A BRIGHTER FUTURE

As we stand at the threshold of an era brimming with unprecedented digital advancements, the journey chronicled in this book offers both a reflection on our remarkable progress and a vision for the path ahead. From the nascent days of the internet to the dawn of artificial intelligence, quantum computing, and beyond, we have witnessed a tapestry of innovation that has fundamentally reshaped our world. But as we gaze into the horizon, the true measure of our journey's success will be determined not just by our technological prowess but by our ability to harness these advancements for the greater good.

The digital age presents us with a unique set of opportunities and challenges, a dual-edged sword that offers the potential to address some of our most pressing global challenges while also urging us to navigate the complexities of ethical considerations, privacy, and the digital divide. As we move forward, it is imperative that we, as a global community, commit to leveraging our innovations and technologies to cultivate a better life for ourselves and for generations to come.

The potential to tackle global challenges such as climate change, healthcare, education, and inequality has never been more within our grasp. The advancements in AI, quantum computing, and the interconnectedness provided by the internet open new avenues for solving complex problems, driving sustainable development, and fostering a more inclusive global society. By prioritising collaboration over competition and empathy over exploitation, we can utilise our digital tools to build resilient communities, advance scientific research, and ensure equitable access to information and resources.

Moreover, as we chart the course toward this brighter future, it is crucial that we remain vigilant stewards of the digital landscape. The ethical use of AI, the protection of personal privacy, and the security of our digital infrastructure must be foundational principles guiding our progress. We must cultivate a digital ecosystem that values transparency, accountability, and inclusivity, ensuring that the benefits of technological advancements are shared broadly and equitably.

In embracing the positive perspectives for the future, it is also essential to recognize the role of individual and collective action in shaping the digital world. Every coder, creator, entrepreneur, and user contributes to the fabric of the digital age. By fostering a culture of innovation that is grounded in ethical considerations and aimed at solving real-world problems, we can ensure that our digital future is one marked by prosperity, security, and opportunity for all.

As we venture into the uncharted territories of the digital frontier, let us carry forward the lessons learned from our past innovations. Let us commit to using our collective ingenuity not just for the pursuit of technological advancement but for the betterment of humanity. In the face of global challenges, our digital tools empower us with the capability to effect meaningful change, to bridge divides, and to create a sustainable, inclusive future.

The journey ahead is filled with potential, a testament to the boundless possibilities that lie within our grasp. By harnessing the power of our innovations with foresight, responsibility, and a shared commitment to the common good, we can indeed build a better life — not just for ourselves but for the next generations that will inherit this world. Let this be our collective mission as we move forward: to ensure that the digital age is remembered not only for its technological marvels but for its contribution to making the world a better place for all.

CHAPTER 22:
THE DIGITAL ODYSSEY CONTINUES

As we stand on the precipice of 2024, peering into the vast expanse of the digital era's latest frontier, we find ourselves at the dawn of a revolution not just technological, but cultural and socio-economic as well. The emergence of quantum computing and the pervasive influence of artificial intelligence (AI) have set the stage for a profound transformation in how we connect, create, and consume.

Quantum computing, once a figment of theoretical physics, has become the beacon of the next internet evolution as we approach 2024. This groundbreaking technology promises to redefine the very fabric of internet technology, offering processing power that dwarfs that of today's most advanced supercomputers. The implications for cybersecurity are monumental, with quantum encryption offering a near-impregnable shield for our digital lives. Yet, this quantum leap also poses new challenges, threatening to render obsolete our current encryption standards and with it, the privacy of digital communications as we know it.

The socio-economic impact of this quantum shift is equally significant. The acceleration of data processing and analysis capabilities holds the promise of solving complex scientific and economic problems, from climate modelling to financial forecasting, at speeds previously unimaginable. This leap forward has the potential to drive innovation and efficiency, heralding a new era of economic growth and environmental stewardship.

By 2025, AI's influence on our lives and businesses is projected to be all-encompassing. Media platforms, leveraging advanced AI algorithms, are set to offer hyper-personalised content, tailoring every aspect of the user experience to individual preferences and behaviours. This evolution in content consumption represents a significant shift in the cultural landscape, where every song, show, or article is a mirror reflecting our unique tastes and interests.

Yet, this AI-driven personalization wave also raises critical questions about privacy and the homogenization of culture. As algorithms narrow our content exposure to match our existing preferences, we risk creating digital echo chambers, insulating us from diverse perspectives and experiences.

The anticipated growth in global internet users to 4.9 billion by 2025 marks a milestone in human connectivity. This surge reflects not merely the spread of technology but the burgeoning recognition of the internet as an essential utility, akin to water or electricity. The socio-economic ramifications are profound, with increased connectivity fostering global trade, education, and cultural exchange, bridging geographic and socio-economic divides like never before.

However, this connectivity also underscores the digital divide that persists, highlighting the disparities in access between urban and rural, affluent and impoverished communities. Bridging this divide becomes not just a technical challenge but a moral imperative, essential for ensuring that the benefits of the digital age are universally accessible.

The digital transformation of the mid-2020s has left its mark on the cultural landscape as well. The rise of virtual reality concerts, offering immersive, multisensory experiences, has redefined live music, allowing artists and fans to connect in ways that transcend physical boundaries. This period has also seen the resurgence of vinyl and analog media, a cultural countercurrent that romanticise the tactile and the tangible amid an increasingly virtual world.

The main marketing trend of this era is the integration of AI into every facet of marketing strategy. From predictive analytics to AI-driven content creation, marketers are now equipped with tools that can anticipate consumer needs, personalise messaging at an individual level, and engage customers in ongoing, dynamic conversations. This AI-driven marketing renaissance represents a shift towards more authentic, personalised brand experiences, challenging companies to maintain a delicate balance between personalization and privacy.

As we navigate through the mid-2020s, we find ourselves at a confluence of technological advancement and cultural evolution. Quantum computing and AI are not merely shaping the future of the internet; they are redefining the human experience. Amid this rapid transformation, we grapple with the ethical, cultural, and socio-economic implications of these technologies, striving to harness their potential while safeguarding the values that define us as a society.

In this chapter of our digital odyssey, we are reminded that progress is not just about the leaps we make but the bridges we build—bridges that connect us to each other, to diverse cultures and perspectives, and to a future where technology amplifies our humanity rather than diminishes it.

CHAPTER 23:
VISION 2028 - AR, BCI, AND THE PULSE OF 6G

Diving into the heart of the late 2020s, we're not just stepping into a new era; we're leaping into a reality where the fabric of daily life is interwoven with threads of augmented reality (AR), mixed reality (MR), brain-computer interfaces (BCI), and the whisper of 6G networks buzzing in the air. It's a world that once lived in the imaginations of sci-fi writers and visionary tech pioneers, now pulsating with life and energy, ready to unfold its stories.

By 2026, AR and MR have ceased to be the playthings of tech enthusiasts, seamlessly integrating into the rhythm of everyday life. Picture this: you're walking through a city street, and the history of every building, the story of every monument, unfolds before your eyes, narrated by holographic guides only you can see. This isn't just about enhanced experiences; it's about education made accessible, about cultural heritage preserved in the digital ether, accessible to all, bridging gaps in knowledge and understanding across societies.

The advent of BCIs (Brain-Computer Interface) and advanced wearable tech by 2027 brings about a revolution in healthcare. Imagine a world where thoughts alone can control prosthetic limbs, where mental health is not just a conversation but a spectrum of care managed through wearable devices that monitor and adjust to your body's needs in real-time. The socio-economic impact is profound, offering independence and support to millions, reducing healthcare costs, and opening new avenues for employment and participation in society for those once sidelined.

Musically, the late 2020s are a renaissance of creativity. Artists harness AR and MR to craft immersive experiences that transcend traditional performances. Concerts are no longer bound by physical venues but are accessible anywhere, anytime, to anyone with a pair of smart glasses or a headset. This era witnesses the rise of virtual music festivals, where the audience, each from their corner of the globe, shares a collective experience that's both intimate and grand, reshaping the communal essence of music consumption and fan interaction.

Culturally, the blend of AR, MR, and wearable tech fosters a new form of storytelling. Interactive theatre takes to the streets, turning the mundane into stages for epic narratives where the audience becomes part of the story, blurring the lines between reality and fiction. Public spaces are transformed into canvases for digital art, accessible through devices that everyone wears as naturally as a pair of glasses, making art and culture a shared, communal experience that enriches the social fabric.

The proliferation of 6G networks by 2028 does more than just speed up our internet connections; it revolutionises the way businesses connect with consumers. The main marketing trend of this period is hyper-personalised, immersive advertising experiences. Imagine walking past a coffee shop and receiving a personalised invite through your AR glasses, offering your favourite brew at a discount, thanks to a quick scan of your digital profile. Or picture a scenario where trying on clothes or testing a new car no longer requires a visit to the store but a moment in your living room, with every detail tailored to your preferences, captured through years of wearable tech gathering your likes, dislikes, and dreams.

This isn't just about selling more; it's about creating value, about making connections that feel personal and genuine in a digital age. Brands that thrive in the late 2020s are those that understand the power of storytelling, of creating experiences that resonate on a personal level, leveraging the ubiquity of AR, MR, and the seamless connectivity of 6G networks to craft messages that speak directly to the heart.

As we navigate through the late 2020s, we find ourselves in a world where technology is no longer a tool but a companion, a canvas for our dreams and aspirations. It's a period of great socio-economic and cultural transformation, driven by advancements that once seemed the realm of fantasy. Yet, amidst this whirlwind of innovation, the core of our journey remains unchanged – the quest to make the world a better place, not just for the few but for everyone, bringing to life the vision shared by pioneers of the past and present.

In this dance of progress and humanity, every step we take is a step towards a future where technology serves not just our needs but our hopes, our dreams, and our collective well-being. Welcome to the late 2020s, where every moment is a glimpse into the future, and every innovation is a bridge to a world we build together, a world of possibilities waiting just beyond the horizon.

CHAPTER 24:
HORIZON 2032 - CRAFTING CONNECTIONS IN THE AGE OF IMMERSIVE REALITIES

Crafting a detailed narrative that encapsulates the transformative journey from 2029 to 2032, while adhering to the constraints and guidelines provided, is a task that beckons us to explore the boundless possibilities on the horizon. Let's embark on this journey together, navigating through a period marked by unprecedented technological advancements and their profound impact on society, culture, and the very fabric of human connection.

As we glide into 2029, the digital landscape is teeming with innovation, but none as captivating as the emergence of autonomous AI content creation. Imagine a world where AI doesn't just assist in the creative process; it leads it, crafting stories, music, and visual art with a depth and nuance indistinguishable from their human-made counterparts. This isn't just about efficiency or novelty; it's a revolution that democratises creativity, making high-quality media accessible to all, irrespective of resources or skills. The socio-economic implications are profound, levelling the playing field for creators across the globe and birthing a new era of cultural diversity in media.

By 2030, virtual reality has ascended from the realms of gaming and niche experiences to become a primary platform for media consumption. VR offers not just immersion but a new dimension of interaction, turning passive viewers into active participants in their entertainment journeys. This shift redefines the landscape of storytelling, offering audiences the chance to live within the narratives they love, transforming storytelling from a one-way street into a sprawling, multi-directional exploration of narrative possibilities.

The milestone of 5.7 billion people connected to the internet by 2030 is more than a statistic; it's a testament to the internet's role as the central nervous system of our global community. This surge in connectivity doesn't just shrink distances; it expands opportunities, knitting together the human tapestry with threads of shared knowledge and empathy. The economic implications are staggering, with digital markets reaching previously untapped populations, spurring innovation, and fostering economic growth in corners of the world once left in the shadows of the digital divide.

The year 2031 marks the advent of fully immersive digital worlds, environments so rich and convincing they rival reality itself. These are spaces where the physical and digital blend, offering experiences that are at once fantastical and deeply personal. From exploring ancient civilizations to living out sci-fi epics, these digital realms offer escape, education, and exploration in equal measure, redefining the concept of "experience" in the process.

By 2032, interactive and adaptive storytelling has reshaped the narrative landscape. Media content is no longer a static offering but a living, breathing entity that responds to and evolves with its audience. This is storytelling that considers your emotions, choices, and even your surroundings, offering a narrative experience that is uniquely yours. The implications for education and empathy are vast, offering unparalleled windows into perspectives and experiences far removed from our own.

The expansion of satellite internet services in 2032 stands as a beacon of hope for bridging the global digital divide. With high-speed, reliable internet reaching the most remote corners of the globe, access to information, education, and economic opportunities is no longer a privilege but a right. This technological leap forward carries the promise of a more equitable world, where geography is no longer a barrier to opportunity.

As we navigate through these transformative years, we witness not just technological evolution but a renaissance of human connection. The emergence of autonomous AI content creation, the ascendancy of VR as a primary media platform, the creation of fully immersive digital worlds, and the democratisation of internet access are not just milestones on a timeline; they are signposts on our journey to a more connected, creative, and empathetic world.

The late 2020s and early 2030s beckon us to envision a future where technology serves not just as a tool for progress but as a canvas for our collective imagination, a bridge to understanding, and a catalyst for global unity. In this chapter of our shared story, we are reminded that the future is not a distant dream but a living, breathing reality that we shape with every innovation, every story, and every connection we forge. Welcome to a world where every individual is not just a spectator but a creator, a participant, and a storyteller in the grand, unfolding narrative of humanity.

CHAPTER 25:
BEYOND THE HORIZON - THE SYMPHONY OF 2036 IN HOLOGRAMS AND HEARTBEATS

Embarking on a journey from 2033 to 2036, we find ourselves in a world where the tapestry of human experience is richly woven with the threads of technological marvels and digital dreams turned into reality. This period stands as a testament to humanity's relentless pursuit of innovation, a time when the realms of science fiction and tangible existence merge, offering a glimpse into a future once imagined, now lived.

As the calendar marks 2033, the air we breathe seems alight with the glow of holographic displays, casting their radiant dance across public spaces worldwide. These aren't just advertisements or information boards; they're canvases of light painting the mundane with the magic of the future. Cities transform into dynamic galleries, where art and information flow freely, accessible to all, turning every corner into an exhibition, every square into a theatre. This isn't just a shift in how we see the world; it's a leap into how we experience and interact with it. The socio-economic impact is profound, democratising access to information and culture, breaking down barriers between art and audience, and opening new avenues for creators and marketers alike.

By 2034, the concept of a personal assistant has evolved beyond mere voice commands and text searches. Neural network-based AI companions become an integral part of daily life, understanding nuances and emotions, adapting to individual needs and preferences with an empathy that blurs the lines between human and machine. This leap in AI capability transforms everyday tasks, making life not just more manageable, but richer, offering personalised insights and freeing time for creativity and connection. The ripple effect on the economy is significant, as businesses adapt to a landscape where consumers are guided by AI with an unprecedented understanding of their desires and needs, reshaping markets and consumer behaviour in ways we're only beginning to comprehend.

2035 arrives with a surge in the global internet user base to 6.5 billion, a milestone that underscores the internet's role as the backbone of modern society. This expansion is not just numerical; it represents a deeper, more intrinsic weave of connectivity into the fabric of daily existence, where access to information, education, and opportunity is seen not as a luxury, but as a fundamental right. Quantum computing begins to mainstream in media processing this year, revolutionising content creation, data analysis, and user experience. This isn't merely about faster computing; it's about creating and consuming media in ways that were previously impossible, opening doors to experiences that are more immersive, interactive, and personalised than ever before.

By the time we reach 2036, the integration of technology with our very biology takes a bold step forward with the development of bio-integrated media devices. These devices promise a future where media consumption is as natural as breathing, where experiences are not just seen and heard but felt, tapping directly into our senses. The implications for how we learn, entertain, and connect with each other are staggering, offering pathways to empathy and understanding that transcend traditional boundaries of communication.

The musical and cultural landscapes of this era are rich with innovation, where holographic concerts bring performances to life in three-dimensional splendour, allowing artists to reach audiences in deeply personal and engaging ways. Virtual reality operas, interactive art installations that respond to the viewer's emotions, and AI-generated symphonies that adapt to the listener's mood, are not just entertainment; they're experiences that challenge and expand our understanding of art and its role in society.

The main marketing trend of this period revolves around hyper-personalised, immersive advertising experiences. With the advent of holographic displays, neural network-based personal assistants, and bio-integrated media devices, marketers have unprecedented tools at their disposal to engage consumers. Advertising becomes less about selling and more about creating value, crafting experiences that resonate on a personal level, leveraging technology to meet consumers in a space of authenticity and engagement.

As we navigate through these transformative years, we're reminded that at the heart of every technological advance is the pursuit of a more connected, understanding, and empathetic world. The journey from 2033 to 2036 is not just about marvelling at the wonders of technology; it's about recognizing the potential these innovations have to make the world a better place for everyone. In this future, every innovation, every leap forward in connectivity and immersive experience, is a step toward bridging divides, fostering creativity, and building a global community united in its diversity. This is a chapter in our shared story where technology becomes a mirror reflecting our collective hopes, dreams, and the infinite possibilities that lie within the human spirit.

CHAPTER 26:
HORIZONS EXPANDED - NAVIGATING THE NEW REALITIES OF 2037-2039

As the world tiptoes from the mid to the late 2030s, we find ourselves not just crossing years but leaping across the boundaries of imagination into a reality once penned down by visionary authors and dreamt by the night sky gazers. The period between 2037 and 2039 is not merely a passage of time; it's a vibrant tapestry of innovation, culture, and connectivity that redefines the essence of human experience.

In 2037, the advent of AI-generated real-time news and reporting marked a pivotal shift in the landscape of media and journalism. This isn't about machines taking over the newsrooms but about augmenting the human capacity to deliver news with unprecedented speed and accuracy. Imagine a world where information is not just timely but tailored, where news reports adapt in real-time to the interests and needs of their audience. This innovation democratises information, making it accessible to all corners of the globe, breaking down barriers of language and geography. The socio-economic impact is profound, offering a more informed global citizenry and fostering a more transparent, accountable media landscape.

By 2038, the creation of personalised media environments will revolutionise the way we consume content. These are not just algorithms suggesting what to watch or listen to next; these are immersive, adaptive spaces that understand your mood, your tastes, and even your aspirations. Whether it's a virtual reality concert that adjusts its setlist to your emotions or a documentary that shifts its focus based on your interests, media consumption becomes an experience uniquely yours. This shift has a ripple effect on culture and society, nurturing a more empathetic, engaged, and culturally diverse global community.

2039 brings us to the cusp of a new frontier with the development of space-based media platforms. As humanity reaches out to the stars, our media follows, offering perspectives that once belonged to the realm of astronauts to anyone with a VR headset. This isn't just about broadcasting from space; it's about creating content that captures the awe and wonder of the cosmos, making the vastness of space feel a little closer to home. The cultural impact is staggering, inspiring a new generation of explorers, scientists, and dreamers, and reminding us all of the tiny, precious blue dot we call home.

Throughout these years, a prevailing marketing trend emerges, centred around the concept of authenticity and personalised connection. In a world awash with content, brands find their voice not through the loudest ads but through stories that resonate on a personal level. Marketing becomes a dialogue, a shared journey between brands and their communities, leveraging the power of AI, personalised media environments, and even space-based platforms to craft experiences that transcend traditional advertising.

As we reflect on this whirlwind of innovation and change, we're reminded of the profound impact technology has on our socio-economic structures, our culture, and our very identity. From AI-driven news that keeps us informed and engaged, to personalised media environments that cater to our every mood, to the boundless potential of space-based media that lifts our gaze to the stars, these years are a testament to human ingenuity and the relentless pursuit of progress.

Yet, amid this awe-inspiring journey, we carry with us a vision - a vision that technology, in all its wonder and complexity, serves as a bridge. A bridge that connects not just minds but hearts, across the vast expanse of space and the intricate web of our global community. It's a vision where every innovation, every leap forward, brings us closer to a world where everyone, regardless of where they are born or the challenges they face, has a seat at the table of the future.

In the story of 2037 to 2039, we don't just see the future; we see a promise—a promise of a world more connected, more vibrant, and more inclusive than ever before. It's a chapter not of technology alone but of humanity's enduring quest to use our tools, our creativity, and our dreams to build a better tomorrow for all.

CHAPTER 27: INTO THE VORTEX - THE 2040S ODYSSEY OF MIND, MEDIA, AND THE GLOBAL MOSAIC

Embarking on a narrative journey from 2040 to 2048, we find ourselves weaving through the tapestry of a world transformed by leaps in technology, each stitch a testament to human ingenuity and the relentless pursuit of making the impossible, possible. This period is not just a timeline of advancements; it's a saga of how these innovations redefine our socio-economic landscapes, enrich our cultural tapestries, and evolve the art of storytelling and connection in the digital age.

As we step into 2040, the world buzzes with the excitement of a groundbreaking revolution in media consumption - the advent of direct neural connections. This isn't about clicking on screens or speaking to voice assistants; it's about experiencing media in the most visceral way imaginable. Imagine feeling the rush of a protagonist in a high-speed chase or the emotional turmoil of a drama, all without moving from your couch. This technology blurs the lines between reality and fiction, making every experience deeply personal and profoundly immersive. Socio-economically, this shift democratises experiences, allowing individuals, regardless of physical ability or geographical location, to explore the world in ways they never thought possible.

By this time, the projection of 7.2 billion people connected online becomes a reality, nearly achieving global internet coverage. This milestone is monumental, not just in its scale but in its implications for global equality and access to information. Education, healthcare, and economic opportunities become more universally accessible, catalysing a wave of global innovation and collaboration previously unseen. The digital divide begins to close, ushering in an era where knowledge and opportunity are not privileges but rights accessible to all.

Moving into 2042, holographic communication becomes the norm, transforming how we interact with each other. Gone are the days of flat, emotionless texts or even video calls. Now, we can sit across from a holographic projection of a friend thousands of miles away, sharing a moment as if in the same room. This technology doesn't just change how we communicate; it reshapes our understanding of presence and intimacy, making every conversation a shared experience, tangible and real.

By 2045, total immersion entertainment systems take the world by storm, offering experiences so real they defy distinction from actuality. These systems integrate seamlessly with our neural connections, allowing us to live within our favourite stories, explore alien worlds, or relive historical events with a fidelity that makes every moment indistinguishable from reality. This era sees a renaissance in storytelling, where creators craft worlds not just to be seen or heard, but to be lived.

In 2048, autonomous AI creativity marks the dawn of a new age of art and innovation. AI systems now possess the capability for independent creative thought, composing symphonies, painting masterpieces, and writing novels that resonate with the depth and complexity of human emotion. This isn't a usurpation of the human role in creativity but an expansion of it, a collaboration between human and machine that pushes the boundaries of art and expression.

Throughout this period, the prevailing marketing trend shifts towards hyper-personalised, experience-driven engagement. Brands no longer sell products or services; they offer experiences, tailored to the individual's desires and emotions, crafted through the deep understanding provided by neural technology and AI. Marketing becomes an art form in itself, creating narratives that resonate on a personal level, forging connections that are meaningful and lasting.

As we navigate through these transformative years, we're reminded of the power of technology not just to change how we live but to enrich how we feel, connect, and dream. From the universal connectivity that binds us closer to the wonders of holographic communication that make every interaction more meaningful, to the immersive worlds that expand our horizons and the creative collaborations that redefine art, this chapter in our collective journey stands as a beacon of what's possible when we dare to imagine and work to realise a future where technology serves not just our needs but our aspirations to make the world a better place for everyone.

In this unfolding saga of progress and possibility, we see not just the future of technology but the ongoing evolution of our shared human experience, a reminder that at the heart of every innovation lies the timeless pursuit of connection, understanding, and the boundless creativity that defines us.

CHAPTER 28: THE DIGITAL DAWN - EMBRACING A CONNECTED HUMANITY (2050-2053)

Crafting a detailed narrative that encapsulates the transformative journey from 2050 to 2053, while adhering to the constraints and guidelines provided, is a task that beckons us to explore the boundless possibilities on the horizon. Let's embark on this journey together, navigating through a period marked by unprecedented technological advancements and their profound impact on society, culture, and the very fabric of human connection.

As the calendar flips to 2050, we find ourselves on the cusp of a new era, one where the digital and physical realms meld more seamlessly than ever before. With 7.9 billion people now connected to the internet, the world has never been more intertwined. This connectivity isn't just about the sheer numbers; it's a reflection of a society where access to information, education, and opportunity is nearly universal—a world where the digital divide has all but vanished, allowing ideas and innovations to flow freely across continents.

In 2051, the introduction of universal digital identity systems marks a pivotal shift in how we navigate our digital lives. Imagine a world where every individual has a secure, unified digital identity that streamlines access to services, simplifies transactions, and enhances privacy. This shift has profound socio-economic implications, dramatically reducing fraud, boosting economic inclusion, and making government services more accessible and efficient. It's a leap toward a future where trust and security form the bedrock of our digital interactions.

By 2052, the healthcare landscape will be revolutionised by the emergence of advanced AI-driven platforms. These systems offer personalised healthcare like never before, predicting health issues before they arise, and providing tailored treatment plans that adapt to each individual's unique physiology. This innovation doesn't just transform healthcare delivery; it reshapes our very approach to wellness, making preventive care and early detection the norms rather than the exceptions. The impact is monumental, significantly reducing healthcare costs and making quality care accessible to underserved communities around the globe.

As we venture into 2053, the expansion of the global quantum network ushers in a new age of internet technology. With the quantum internet becoming more accessible, we're not just talking about faster speeds or more secure connections; we're looking at a complete overhaul of how data is transmitted and processed. This quantum leap forward enhances everything from secure communications to complex computing tasks, opening up new frontiers in research, finance, and cybersecurity. It's a testament to human ingenuity and a glimpse into a future where our digital infrastructure is as boundless as our ambition.

Throughout these transformative years, a prevailing marketing trend emerges, centred around the concept of authenticity and personalised connection. In a world awash with content, brands find their voice not through the loudest ads but through stories that resonate on a personal level. Marketing becomes a dialogue, a shared journey between brands and their communities, leveraging the power of AI, personalised media environments, and even space-based platforms to craft experiences that transcend traditional advertising.

As we navigate through these transformative years, we're reminded that at the heart of every technological advance is the pursuit of a more connected, understanding, and empathetic world. From AI-driven news that keeps us informed and engaged, to personalised media environments that cater to our every mood, to the boundless potential of space-based media that lifts our gaze to the stars, these years are a testament to human ingenuity and the relentless pursuit of progress.

Yet, amid this awe-inspiring journey, we carry with us a vision - a vision that technology, in all its wonder and complexity, serves as a bridge. A bridge that connects not just minds but hearts, across the vast expanse of space and the intricate web of our global community. It's a vision where every innovation, every leap forward, brings us closer to a world where everyone, regardless of where they are born or the challenges they face, has a seat at the table of the future.

In this chapter of our shared story, we don't just see the future; we see a promise—a promise of a world more connected, more vibrant, and more inclusive than ever before. It's a chapter not of technology alone but of humanity's enduring quest to use our tools, our creativity, and our dreams to build a better tomorrow for all.

CHAPTER 29: NAVIGATING THE 2050S' NEW FRONTIERS

As dawn breaks in 2054, the digital heartbeat of the planet pulses stronger than ever, with 8.5 billion souls woven into the vast network of global connectivity. This isn't just about more people logging on; it's a testament to the internet's evolution into a fundamental human right, accessible to every corner of the globe. The socio-economic landscape is transformed, with digital inclusion breaking down barriers to education, healthcare, and economic opportunities, empowering individuals and communities in ways previously unimaginable.

In this era, the symbiosis between AI and the human brain marks a watershed moment in our evolution. By 2055, enhancements in cognitive capabilities are not the stuff of science fiction but a reality that elevates human potential. This fusion of technology and biology enhances creativity, problem-solving, and learning, paving the way for innovations that leapfrog generations. The impact on the workforce is profound, as skills and jobs evolve to meet the needs of this new paradigm, fostering a socio-economic environment where adaptability and creativity become the currency of success.

As we journey through 2056, environmental control technologies emerge as the heroes of our time. Harnessing the power of advanced AI and quantum computing, humanity takes a bold step forward in addressing the existential threat of climate change. These technologies enable precise manipulation of weather patterns, carbon capture at unprecedented scales, and the restoration of ecosystems, redefining our relationship with the planet. This isn't just an environmental victory; it's an economic revolution, birthing new industries and revitalising old ones, united by the common goal of sustainable coexistence with our world.

The year 2057 heralds the dawn of fully autonomous societies, where AI systems manage everything from traffic flows to energy distribution, healthcare, and even governance. This transition to a society where decisions are made based on data, efficiency, and the collective good challenges our traditional notions of autonomy and authority. Yet, it also offers a glimpse into a future of unparalleled harmony and efficiency, where human ingenuity is freed to explore the bounds of creativity and innovation.

Throughout this period, the cultural landscape vibrates with the energy of a new renaissance. Music and the arts flourish, powered by AI collaborations that push the boundaries of expression and experience. Holographic concerts featuring AI-generated symphonies play to global audiences, while virtual reality art galleries host exhibitions that are as much about exploring new worlds as they are about viewing paintings or sculptures. These cultural milestones reflect a society deeply entwined with technology, yet fervently exploring the quintessence of human emotion and creativity.

The prevailing marketing trend of this era is deeply personal and immersive, leveraging the ubiquitous connectivity and AI insights to create campaigns that resonate on a personal level like never before. Brands no longer sell products or services; they curate experiences, crafting narratives that align with individual values and aspirations, delivered through immersive platforms that engage the senses and the mind. This shift to experience-based marketing reflects a deeper understanding of the human psyche, where authenticity and relevance become the pillars of engagement.

As we reflect on this journey from 2054 to 2057, it becomes clear that we are not just passive observers of change but active participants in shaping a future where technology serves as a bridge to a more inclusive, creative, and sustainable world. This chapter in our collective story is about more than the marvels of technology; it's a narrative of human resilience, aspiration, and the unyielding pursuit of a better tomorrow for all.

In this unfolding saga of the late 2050s, we witness a world in transformation, a testament to the enduring spirit of innovation and the boundless potential of human-AI collaboration. It's a reminder that the future is not a destination but a journey, one that we navigate together, propelled by the shared dream of a world where every individual has the opportunity to thrive.

CHAPTER 30:
NAVIGATING THE DIGITAL
COSMOS OF 2058-2060

Embarking on a narrative journey from 2058 to 2060, we traverse a landscape where the bounds of human ingenuity stretch into the cosmos, and the essence of individual experience is redefined by the gentle caress of technology. These years are not merely ticks on the timeline of progress; they're bold strokes on the canvas of our shared future, painting a world where connection, creativity, and innovation intertwine in the dance of the digital age.

As the dawn of 2058 breaks, humanity takes a monumental leap with the expansion of internet infrastructure to other planets. This isn't just about sending emails from Mars or streaming the Earthrise from the Moon; it's a profound expansion of the human domain, knitting the fabric of our communities across the vacuum of space. The socio-economic implications are as vast as the universe itself, opening new frontiers for research, development, and even interplanetary commerce. This leap into the cosmos brings with it a new era of collaboration and discovery, uniting us in our quest to explore the unknown and in doing so, bringing us closer together, even as we journey far from our terrestrial cradle.

By 2059, the development of AI-enhanced personal reality devices marks another milestone in our technological odyssey. These devices, more intimate than any technology we've known, tailor our perception of reality, enhancing it with information, beauty, and insights tailored to our individual needs and desires. Imagine walking through a city, seeing not just the streets and buildings of the present, but layers of history, art, and data woven into your vision, enriching every glance with a tapestry of knowledge and sensation. This innovation transcends mere convenience, offering a lens through which the richness of the world is magnified, personalised, and made accessible to all, redefining the very essence of experience.

As the decade closes in 2060, global connectivity reaches a new zenith, with 9.0 billion people connected. This milestone is a testament to the democratisation of access, where the internet becomes as fundamental as air or water, a utility that powers not just our homes and industries, but our dreams and aspirations. The socio-economic impact of this universal connectivity is profound, erasing the digital divide and empowering individuals with the tools to learn, create, and contribute to the global tapestry, regardless of geography or circumstance.

Throughout this period, the cultural landscape vibrates with the energy of innovation. Music, now created and experienced in multi-sensory formats, transcends auditory boundaries, offering immersive experiences that engage all the senses, connecting artists and audiences in a shared digital embrace that defies the limits of space and time. Cultural highlights include virtual reality concerts that transport audiences to fantastical realms, and AI collaborations that produce art and music resonating with the complexity and depth of human emotion, yet born from the silicon heart of machines.

The prevailing marketing trend of this era is the seamless integration of brand experiences into the fabric of personal reality. Marketing becomes not just a matter of exposure but of experience, crafting narratives and interactions that are woven into the personal realities created by AI-enhanced devices. Brands that succeed are those that understand this intimate new landscape, offering not just products or services, but enhancements to the personal reality of each individual, making every interaction meaningful and every experience resonant.

As we look back on the journey from 2058 to 2060, we see more than a chronicle of technological milestones; we see a saga of human aspiration and creativity, a narrative of how our tools and dreams converge to create a world that is more connected, more vibrant, and more inclusive. In this future, technology serves not just to bridge distances or augment realities, but to weave the vast and varied threads of human experience into a shared story of progress and possibility.

This chapter, then, is not just a glimpse into the future; it is a reflection on the power of human ingenuity and the enduring spirit of exploration that propels us forward. It is a testament to our collective journey toward a future where every individual has the opportunity to explore, create, and connect, forging a world that reflects the best of what we can imagine and the best of who we are.

CHAPTER 31:
WEAVING THE PAST, PRESENT, AND FUTURE

As we draw the curtain on this odyssey through time, from the embryonic whispers of the internet in the 1960s to the pulsating digital cosmos of 2060, it's hard not to pause and marvel at the journey we've traversed together. Through pages steeped in the evolution of connectivity, we've witnessed humanity's boundless capacity for innovation, its insatiable curiosity, and its unwavering pursuit of progress. This narrative, woven from the threads of socio-economic transformation, cultural renaissance, and marketing revolutions, is more than a history; it's a testament to the indomitable spirit of human collaboration and creativity.

Reflecting on the socio-economic fabric of our shared digital future, we've seen how the internet's expansion to 9.0 billion souls by 2060 has not just bridged distances but has dismantled barriers, knitting the world into a tighter community. This universal connectivity has democratised access to knowledge, opportunity, and innovation, paving the way for a future where the digital divide is a relic of the past, and the global economy thrives on the principles of inclusivity and equity.

Culturally, the journey has been nothing short of a renaissance, a celebration of human expression amplified by the digital medium. From the holographic concerts that brought artists into our living rooms to the AI collaborations that pushed the boundaries of art and music, we've seen a fusion of technology and creativity that has enriched the human experience, making culture a shared, immersive, and interactive tapestry accessible to all.

In the realm of marketing, the evolution has been profound,

moving from the broadcast methods of the past to the hyper-personalised, experience-driven engagements of the future. This shift towards creating meaningful, resonant connections between brands and individuals has redefined the essence of marketing, highlighting the power of authenticity and personalization in a world awash with digital content.

As we stand at the threshold of what's to come, it's with a heart full of gratitude that I extend my deepest thanks to you, dear reader, for embarking on this journey with me. Your curiosity, your enthusiasm, and your hunger for understanding the digital tapestry that binds our world have been the guiding stars of this narrative. This book, while an exploration of the past and a speculation on the future, is ultimately a reflection of our collective journey through the age of the internet—a journey defined by our shared triumphs, challenges, and aspirations.

In the spirit of the open, interconnected world that the internet has fostered, I invite you to continue this conversation beyond the pages of this book. Share your thoughts, your visions for the future, and your reflections on how the digital age has shaped our world. You can reach out via my social media channels, where the dialogue that began in these pages can flourish and grow, enriched by the diverse perspectives and insights of a global community.

As we look to the horizon, let us carry forward the lessons of the past and the dreams of the future with humility and hope. Let us strive to ensure that the digital age remains a force for good, a tool for empowerment, and a canvas for the boundless creativity of the human spirit. May the story of the internet, from its humble beginnings to its future possibilities, inspire us to envision a world where technology serves not just our needs but our highest aspirations for a connected, compassionate, and creative humanity.

Thank you for being a part of this journey. Here's to the next chapter, to the untold stories and unexplored possibilities that lie ahead. May we navigate the future with the same spirit of adventure and collaboration that has brought us this far, and may the digital age continue to be a testament to the best of what we can achieve together.

Wishing you the best of thoughts and eager to hear your feedback, let's keep the conversation going. The future is ours to shape, together.

ABOUT THE AUTHOR

Gustavo Morale

 By the age of 25, in 2006, Gustavo Morale demonstrated remarkable foresight and entrepreneurial acumen by co-founding one of the world's first professional ad networks. This pioneering platform reached over 130 million readers monthly, supporting for more than 10 years 35,000 publishers, bloggers and content creators, showcasing ad campaigns among many other innovations. Gustavo's relentless pursuit of knowledge, combined with his experience in digital media, advertising, and AdTech, underscores his role as a continuous learner and innovator. His ventures into business, creative projects, marketing, and content creation further solidify his status as a versatile specialist and visionary in the digital era.

www.ingramcontent.com/pod-product-compliance
Lightning Source LLC
LaVergne TN
LVHW051537050326
832903LV00033B/4296